©Marcia Lee Laycock, July 2017

Small Pond Press
Box 637 Blackfalds
Alberta Canada
T0M 0J0

smallpond@telus.net

Love In The Room

All rights reserved. The author guarantees all contents are original and do not infringe upon the legal rights of any other person or work. No part of this book may be used or reproduced, stored in a retrieval system or transmitted in any form or by any means without prior written permission of the publisher, except in the case of brief quotations embodied in critical articles and reviews.

First Edition
Published by Small Pond Press

Introduction

Christmas is a time of divine revelation, divine moments when we all pause, remember, and ponder. I hope you will be blessed by these short meditations on the birth of our Lord.

These devotionals were originally published in local newspapers and magazines and a few in anthologies.

The poem, The Paper Gift, is used with permission of the author.

Love In The Room

Paper Gift
By Mary Elizabeth Lauzon

Hang my words
Fron the tree of life,
Creator,
That I might birth with you,
Fresh as a child,
Glossy ornaments of truth,
Gleaming as all creation
As You.

Table of Contents

Christmas is for Kids	6
Same Old, Same Old?	8
Beauty in Darkness	10
An Unusual Symbol	12
An Appropriate Quote	14
Do You See?	16
Just the Right Gift	20
A Buffer Against the Unexpected	23
Flash Mobs at Christmas	25
Love In the Room	27
A Perfect Choice	29
No Matter What	32
Can Anything Good …	35
It's That Time of Year	37
Pretty Packages	39
Artificial Light	41
Enough	43
Rejoicing in the Present	45
Beginnings and Endings	47
Letting Go	49
How Do You Picture the Christ?	51
Too Much Christmas	53
Wishing I Could Be Jesus	55
The Only Gift We Need	57
Thoughts on Christmas Kitsch	59
The Promise of Christmas	61
God's Gifts	63
Window Shopping	65
A Baby in a Box	67
The Week After	69
To Resolve or Not to Resolve	71
Future Tense	73
About the Author	75

Love In The Room

Christmas is For Kids

My mother always said, "Christmas is for kids." She'd make that statement several times every Christmas season. When we "kids" got older it seemed to be kind of a hint that we were too big for all the fanfare and fuss. But I always thought to myself, *oh good, I get to act like a kid again!* I suppose, in a way, my mother was right. It's the kids who generate the excitement, the kids who take delight in all the presents and decorations. And sometimes it's the kids who teach us what Christmas should be all about. Now that I'm an adult, watching little ones in the shops and malls is a delight because they are so enthralled with everything they see. They seem to see all the tinsel and glitter as though it were silver and gold. They seem to have the ability to just believe in all the wonder and mystical possibilities of Christmas.

We recently watched the classic Christmas movie, *Elf*. The story is about a man who was raised by Santa's elves and goes in search of his real father when he finally learns he's human. (A little suspension of disbelief is obviously needed by adult viewers). The story is about a man with a child's heart. Everything delights him. Of course, he slams up against the cynicism of the real world, time and again, but he manages to keep his child-like innocence and eventually manages to affect change in the hearts of the cynical adults around him.

Having a child's heart isn't only a prerequisite for enjoying Christmas, it's also a prerequisite for belonging to the kingdom of God. Jesus said so Himself in the book of Luke, chapter 18, verse 16 – "Let the little children come to me and do not hinder them, for the kingdom of God belongs to such as these. I tell you the truth, anyone who will not receive the kingdom of God like a little child will never enter it."

What is it that children have that we must have, in order to gain this kingdom? Their innocence, certainly; their willingness to accept that there is someone bigger than them who knows better; their immediate outpouring of love in response to love bestowed on them; their unabashed willingness to tell others what they believe, even if those others scoff.

And most of all, their wholehearted, unreserved faith. Children believe with their whole heart, their whole mind, their whole strength. It's not something they have to force or work at, they just let it happen. They receive the love and forgiveness intended for them and then act accordingly. Oh, to be a child again! To open our hearts to God's love and then let it pour out, that's the message of Christmas we all need to receive. Yes, Christmas is for kids. And we all get to be kids again. Maybe, if we start today, it will last all year long.

Love In The Room

Same Old, Same Old?

It's that time of year again, the time when we begin asking one another, "What do you want for Christmas?" My daughter asked her dad that question the other day and his answer was predictable. "Well, I could use a pair of gloves, maybe some socks and a tie."

Meagan groaned. "I don't want to get you the same old things, Dad," she complained. "That's too boring." Spence tried to come up with something a little more interesting, but so far, gloves and socks are still at the top of the list.

This is also the time when we begin hearing all the same old Christmas carols, receiving all the same old cards, seeing all the same old decorations, baking all the same old cookies and even pulling out the same old (plastic) Christmas tree. Same old, same old. It can all seem so familiar that we forget why we do it. We forget that Christmas has significance, not just because of the holidays and the presents but because of what really happened just a little over two thousand years ago.

The very first Christmas was a time of new things. A new star appeared in the sky and kings from the East recognized it as a sign of something momentous. Angels appeared to shepherds who were shaken from their same old routines and were filled with new hope. Two parents experienced the joy and pain of new life. The birth of Jesus, that event we celebrate on Christmas day, was the beginning of something new for all of us. It was the beginning of reconciliation with God, the beginning of joy and hope and the beginning of true peace.

Unfortunately, we have not yet appropriated all that Christmas means. We have surrounded it with all the trappings of tradition and commercialism but we have failed to claim its true significance. We reject the offer of reconciliation, we refuse the joy, spurn the hope and deny the peace. Then we look around at our corrupt and chaotic world, and we wonder why things are in such turmoil; why do we keep making all the same old mistakes?

Hundreds of years before the birth of the New King, a wise prophet told the people about Him. He foretold His birth, outlined His life and, in great detail, described His death. Isaiah said – "The people walking in darkness have seen a great light. On those living in the land of the shadow of death a light has dawned." We have been living in the shadow of death since the beginning of time and since that moment God planned to dispel that darkness. The light Isaiah speaks of is Jesus Christ.

Christmas doesn't have to be all about the same old stuff. It can be a time filled with joy, hope and peace. It can be a time to embrace the new life Jesus offers.

Love In The Room

Beauty in the Darkness

Winter has landed here, its cold hard boot slamming down on the country and its inhabitants with the force of a sledge hammer. We had been lulled into thinking it wouldn't hit so hard this year. We'd only had a skiff of snow and a few days of chill, but nothing to be concerned about. So this icy blast is a bit of a jolt to us all. How quickly we forget the true face of winter, it's harsh landscape and bitter winds.

As I peer out my front window I shiver and pull my sweater tighter around me. The sun is just setting, the darkness dropping quickly behind the homes on the other side of the pond. It has caught a skater unaware. She continues to glide and weave across the small space as the light fades. And then it happens. Just for a moment the horizon glows, the light shimmers on the ice, the skater is thrown into a silhouette of fluid movement. And the beauty of it takes my breath away.

I am reminded that beauty is always there, just waiting to reveal itself, waiting to slip out of the darkness. I am blessed that I was there, in that moment, to see it, to be struck by it and to give thanks for it. It makes me realize that a big part of being a believer in Christ involves watching, waiting for the beauty. It is ours to bring these moments to light, to make them known to the world. We are the observers, the recorders, the ones who point and say, "Oh, look! Look!"

There is a great need for us to show the way to beauty in the world today, in the face of the images of wreck and ruin we constantly see in the media. There is no greater need for it than now. There is no greater need than for the world to know that beauty exists, that Christ was born to bring it back to us, to elevate it to the holy place where it was intended to be, because all beauty comes from the Father above, through His Son.

Interesting, isn't it, that the place of Jesus' birth was likely not considered beautiful? It was a common, homely place. Some would even have said insignificant. But then there were those moments – the moment when that brightest of stars stopped over the spot where the Christ child lay, the moment when the angels revealed themselves in the skies near Bethlehem, the moment when their voices peeled out with the good news of His birth, the moment when kings bowed down and presented him with gold, frankincense and myrrh.

As we celebrate Christmas once again, let us all be watchful, waiting for those moments when The Christ is revealed through the beauty of this world. Let us all receive the blessing of those moments and then shout, "Oh, look! Look!"

Love In The Room

An Unusual Symbol of Christmas

It was many weeks before Christmas, but Bob was already adamant. He would have no Christmas tree in his home. It wasn't that he was a "bah, humbug," kind of person; on the contrary, Bob was one of those people who seemed to have the Christmas spirit most of the year. But he was also against cutting down a tree, just for the sake of tradition. I thought his idea a bit extreme. How can you have a decent Christmas without a tree? Bob didn't argue, he just remained steadfast in his opinion.

Then, one afternoon, he was seen lugging a large planter into his home. He bought potting soil, filled the pot to the brim and began to move it from place to place in his small living room. When the planter seemed to have found a permanent spot, Bob planted a skinny branch in the middle of the dark soil.

"What's this?" I asked when visiting, "some kind of organic coat rack?" Bob just smiled and replied, "You'll see."

As Christmas approached, Bob bought a set of small white lights and adorned the stick. By this time his "tree" had become a joke among those who knew him. "Nice tree, Bob," they'd say, not bothering to disguise their sarcasm. Bob didn't seem perturbed. He bought a few small decorations and added them to the lights. A few days before Christmas, a small group gathered in his kitchen to celebrate the season. We enjoyed a feast, then were ushered into the living room. It was in darkness but for the small white lights adorning Bob's tree. As we entered the room, a hush fell.

The tree was blooming. Tiny bright green leaves adorned every branch and seemed to glow with life. It had been several dreary Yukon months since we had seen the colour green and the effect was startling. Almost in awe, we could not take our eyes away from that tree, with its tiny green shoots and sparkling white lights.

Bob's tree still glows in my memory. When I think of it now, I realize what a fitting symbol it was of Christmas. It was a bare and homely thing, like the place into which Jesus was born. ("She wrapped him in cloths and laid him in a manger" - Luke 2:7) It appeared ugly, a thing of ridicule and disgrace, like Jesus Himself when he fulfilled His destiny and hung on a cross. ("Those who passed by hurled insults at him ..." - Mark 15:29) Yet Bob's tree was the source of life, of freshness and blessing in the midst of a cold grey winter, just as Jesus, the Messiah, is the source of new life for us all. ("Instead of the thorn bush, will grow the pine tree, and instead of briers the myrtle will grow. This will be for the Lord's renown, for an everlasting sign, which will not be destroyed" (Isaiah 55:13).

Love In The Room

An Appropriate Quote

I read the email with a bit of anticipation and a bit of dread. It was an invitation to another Christmas party. That meant another pot-luck item to prepare, another Chinese auction gift to bring. And I couldn't stop sneezing, so who knew if I'd be well enough to attend. It was almost enough to make me want to shout, "Bah Humbug!" But the instructions in this email piqued my interest. For the gift exchange, we were to bring a favourite quote, done up in some kind of creative way. The favourite quote part would be easy, I thought. I have a huge file of quotes on my computer. With the state of my health, I knew the creative part might be a bit more difficult, but I decided to rise to the challenge.

I clicked into my quotes file and began to read, and read, and read. Nothing seemed exactly right. I was thinking Christmas, but couldn't find anything seasonal. I thought inspirational, but nothing seemed to hit the mark. I thought humorous, but couldn't find anything that made me laugh out loud. So I gave up, swallowed some more cough medicine and went to bed.

The next day I opened the file again. A quote seemed to beam its way to me immediately. It was short but thought provoking, and when I thought about it, the words, from poet Anne Sexton, were very appropriate for the Christmas season. She said: "Put your ear down close to your soul and listen hard."

In the midst of the rush to shop, to bake, to decorate and make it to all those Christmas parties, God is calling us to do just that. He wants us to stop and hear His voice in the tumult. It is a still small voice, but one that echoes with everything we need. It is the voice of a child crying from a manger, the voices of angels singing and shepherds jabbering about a baby born to be King. It is a voice weeping for those in pain and sickness. It is a voice mourning for those who refuse to hear Him. It is a voice shouting victory over the forces of evil and death. And it is a voice calling us to know Him, to know His love for us, love that grants us one more day of life, filled with all its challenges and blessings. Listen for Him. He has promised that anyone Awho hears my voice and opens the door, I will come in and eat with him, and he with me" (Rev.3:20). Not only that, He has promised to stay with you forever, to guide and protect you, and to give you peace.

So, "put your ear down close to your soul and listen hard." You might just hear the true voice of Christmas.

Love In The Room

Do You See?

The women laughed and frowned as they handed the large Christmas stocking from one to another. It was our annual "Warm Up to Winter" Event and it was obvious the game I had picked was a hit.

It entailed putting different items in a Christmas stocking - things that are essential to making Christmas perfect. The stocking is then passed around and everyone tries to guess what's in it. The catch is they can't look. They are only allowed to feel the outside of the stocking and try to figure out what the items are.

As I thought about the game and the items I would put in the stocking, I began to think of all the things pertaining to Christmas that we think are essential. The tree, for instance, gleaming with baubles and tinsel; the lights trimming our homes and businesses; the presents brightly wrapped and kept secret until the 25th; and of course the food – what would Christmas be without the turkey and all its trimmings?

I thought of how all these things can be a distraction from the real message of Christmas and I wondered how I could connect them in my mind with the truth.

I thought about the tree. There wouldn't have

been any scotch pines or blue spruce in Bethlehem, but I remembered a day many years ago when I was cross-country skiing through an evergreen forest. I'd skied hard for a while, so stopped to rest for a moment. Suddenly I
was enthralled by the deep silence and the beauty all around me. A fresh snow had layered the tall trees and a few large flakes were still falling gently from the sky. I was surrounded by Christmas trees, not trimmed in decorations and tinsel, but in the beauty of God's own creation. Every time I see a Christmas tree I can thank him for that tremendous gift – the gift of this world with all its variety and beauty, the gift of those moments when we are still enough to see.

And I thought about the lights – some coloured and twinkling, some large and garish, others tiny and white. And I remembered that Jesus called himself the Light of the world in John 8:12. Psalm 119:130 says "The entrance of your words gives light" and Isaiah 60:1 tells us to "Arise, shine, four your light has come." Isaiah says the Lord will be our "everlasting light." John calls Jesus the true light that gives light and Ephesians 5:8 tells us we ourselves are "now light in the Lord."

One of my favourite missionary stories from Papua New Guinea is about a group of men who came and asked about this Jesus, because, they said they could see the change in their neighbours who had become believers. "They have light in their eyes," they said, "Tell us how to have that light."

Love In The Room

And what about the presents? Well, that's an easy one isn't it? Jesus himself was God's gift to us, the gift that 'keeps on giving' because once we have sought his forgiveness and accepted the sacrifice he made for us, He lives in us. That is a gift that can never been taken away, a gift that out does all others. A gift that should not be kept secret. And we can see the evidence of that gift.

When I became a believer in Christ, the change in me was so obvious people began to comment on it. There were two women who attended the mission church where we went. They usually went south for the winter and when they came into the post office, where I worked, that next spring, they had an argument. You see Sally thought I was the person who had been there in the fall. Betty was convinced it could not be. Then they came to church that Sunday and there I was. They looked at one another and laughed. Now they knew it was me – a new me.

The scripture that says, "if anyone is in Christ, he is a new creation, the old has gone, the new has come!" was a visible truth in me. I was no longer that miserable grouchy postal employee, I was now a child of God who knew she was loved and accepted by a merciful God.

And the food? How can we connect turkey and dressing and mashed potatoes to the truth of Christmas? Food too is God's gift to us, isn't it? I received an interesting email a while ago that listed various foods and what they do for our bodies. The interesting part was that the very shape of the fruits and vegetables can tell us what they do. The carrot, for instance, when sliced looks like the iris of an eye, and its vitamins help keep our eyes healthy. A walnut resembles the human brain and has long been known to help stimulate memory and aid in brain function. The list went on and on and I was amazed at how God has not only given us all that we need, but given us clues on how to use it to the greatest benefit.

And the Lord himself is our food, our nourishment, our sustenance. He said himself, "I am the bread of life."

As I began to connect all the trappings of Christmas to the truth of Christmas, I realized that it's just a matter of seeing what is really in front of us, and connecting it to the mercy and love of Christ. Then we will indeed, truly see.

Love In The Room

Just the Right Gift

My family starts thinking about Christmas at Thanksgiving because that's when we are usually all together and can "pick names," selecting the person we will buy for that year. We started using the wish list method a few years ago, to make the buying easier. Everyone sends their lists to me and I send them out to the rest of the family.

I always enjoy reading the lists - it's quite interesting how everyone's personality comes out in the things they ask for. For instance, one of my sons-in-law is usually quite specific about his requests - it's not just a pair of socks, it's a pair of black socks made of a certain blend of material and patterned in a certain way. This year item number one was a series of baseball trading cards. I shook my head when I read it. Where on earth would we ever find such a thing?

About two weeks after receiving his list I participated in a fund-raiser for a local group. They had a silent auction as well as a number of booths set up with all kinds of Christmas gift ideas. I sighed as I wandered among them, wishing I could get some of my shopping done, but not too hopeful about finding what was on those lists. Then I saw it

- a small sign - "Baseball Trading Cards." I blinked and stepped closer. There were a few packs of cards along with a book. Not knowing anything about baseball, I hesitated. What if these weren't the cards he wanted? What if I had to make a high bid and it was a disappointment to him?

Then I felt that little nudge in my spirit. "This is a gift. Just accept it." I took a step closer. I wrote down my name and put a dollar amount beside it. When I won the item, I sighed again. Even if the dates on the cards were wrong, at least my son-in-law would know I tried to get him what he wanted.

When I got home later that day I immediately went to my computer and looked at the Christmas lists. I sat back in stunned wonder when I read that number one item my son-in-law had listed. The dates on the cards I had won were exactly the dates he wanted! Then I smiled. I couldn't stop thinking about the look on his face when he opens that present. I knew he would be "over-the-moon" happy.

Then I thought about that nudge when I hesitated to put a bid on the auction sheet. "This is a gift. Just accept it."

That's what God the Father says to the world every year at Christmas time. He presents His Son, the one who died for the sins of this sad weary world, and says, this is my gift to you, accept Him. All we have to do is admit we need the sacrifice that happened over 2000 years ago, because we all

Love In The Room

have sinned and continue to "fall short" as the book of Romans 3:23 says. Because Jesus gives us the wondrous gift of His righteousness we are able to sign our names into the book of life and accept what He offers - eternal life with Him. It's why we celebrate His birth - the birth of Jesus who was sent to die for us all.

  This is a gift. Just accept it.

A Buffer Against the Unexpected

"We've had it so easy. This is a shock to the system." I've heard several people voice this thought in the past week. The plunge in the temperatures and the sudden heavy snowfall has left us all shivering and shaking. It's not that we weren't expecting winter. It's just that it seemed to happen all of a sudden.

Life is often like that. Things are going well, then all of a sudden everything changes. A man who has never been sick a day in his life suddenly lands in hospital with a serious illness. A family whose business has always been stable suddenly finds themselves facing bankruptcy. A woman who always thought her husband loved her suddenly has to walk into a divorce court. The unexpected is always just around the corner and it's always a shock to the system.

That's why we all need an anchor, something that will remain constant when life threatens to turn our boat upside down. We need something we can hang onto, something that gives us hope. That anchor came in the form of a small baby born in a stable in an obscure town on the other side of the world. His name is Jesus and he grew into a man who was the saviour of the world. We'll be celebrating His

Love In The Room

birthday soon and for some of us, the hope of Christmas is a desperate need.

The good news is that we can depend on that hope, the hope of eternal life with Christ, the hope of His Spirit living in us here and now. When we have faith in Christ,
the world can throw storm after storm our way. The boat may be battered and tossed about, but it will not sink. The anchor will hold. Jesus is a buffer against the unexpected. He is the one constant in a world where everything can change in an instant.

God's existence and His desire to be involved with us personally is a mystery to us, but it is a mystery that has captured the hearts and minds of millions because they have come to know it is true. It is a truth that has been proclaimed by men and women throughout the ages. Some have spent their entire lives proclaiming it. Some have died because they did. It is a message worth living and dying for. It is the message of Christmas – "For to us a child is born, to us a son is given, and the government will be on his shoulders and he will be called Wonderful Counselor, Mighty God, Everlasting Father, Prince of Peace" (Isaiah 9:6).

When we grab hold of that hope, when we hold on to Jesus, there is nothing that can shake us, not even life's unexpected challenges and disasters. Jesus is our anchor. The anchor will always hold.

Flash Mobs at Christmas

I love the videos of flash mobs that circulate on YouTube and Facebook, especially at this time of year. I love to watch the faces of those in the malls or city squares as they realize that something unusual is happening. The looks range from bemused delight to open-mouthed awe. Cell phones quickly appear to capture the event and the applause at the end is usually long and loud.

What is it about these spontaneous events that delight us?

We aren't expecting it. Who expects a symphony orchestra to suddenly strike up in a food court? The people doing it look just like us yet they are doing something out of the ordinary, something fun and sometimes spectacular. Ordinary routines are suddenly halted, an ordinary day is turned into a festival and the focus on scurrying around to shop is forgotten. Strangers smile at one another and share the delight of discovery. For a few moments, a community is created.

As I watched a video of a flash mob the other day I thought of how perfectly it exemplified the spirit of Christmas.

Love In The Room

Who expected the Messiah to be born as a baby in a manger? The people involved were ordinary people who looked just like all the others in that era yet they were involved in a world-changing event – something totally out of the ordinary, something spectacular. The ordinary routines of Mary and Joseph, the shepherds and the wise men were suddenly halted. An ordinary event, the birth of a child, on an ordinary day, became the pivot on which history would turn. Those who came to worship the Christ child on that day were strangers to one another, but they became companions in a journey that would lead them to the most important discovery of their lives and a joy that would never leave them.

As I thought about it, I thought about my own attitude to yet another Christmas season. I've seen over six decades of them. Yes, I'm that old! And sometimes I miss the delight and the joy I had as a child, because it is all so familiar. It's all so commercial with the constant pressure to buy and my jaded attitude causes me to miss the glory.

Perhaps that's why I love the flash mobs. They renew my joy in this season, they renew my delight in the story that is still the pivot of the world's history even after more than 2,000 years. "For to us a child is born, to us a son is given … And he will be called Wonderful Counsellor, Mighty God, Everlasting Father, Prince of Peace." Isaiah 9:6

Love In the Room

A little boy named Bobby is purported to have said - "Love is what's in the room with you at Christmas if you stop opening presents and listen."

When I read that quote I wondered about what that little boy would hear. The laughter of his siblings, the chatter of the adults; the snoring of his grandfather asleep in his favourite chair perhaps, or the cooking preparations going on in the kitchen; the whine of a new puppy or the mechanical sounds of electronic gifts already opened?

Or perhaps that young and obviously very discerning little boy was hearing something more ethereal. Perhaps he was hearing angels singing praises to the Christ Child, or the words of the Magi as they presented their gifts. Perhaps he was hearing the booming voice of our heavenly Father announcing the arrival of his Son on this earth. Or the voice of Jesus Himself, saying, "Come to me all you who are weary and burdened and I will give you rest" (Matthew 11:28).

Those are indeed the sounds of love, a love so deep, it is impossible to comprehend it. And that Love is present with us, in the room, because the

Love In The Room

Child whose birth we celebrate embodies love and gave us the greatest gift of all time, through a sacrifice performed on a cross in a tiny country in the Middle East over 2,000 years ago.

That little boy knew the secret to finding that Love. It's a matter of shifting our focus from earthly things to things spiritual. In the rush and flurry of the Christmas season it's easy to forget the fact that it is, in its essence, a spiritual time. It's a time to reflect on the birth of a Saviour, a time to ponder our relationship with Him, a time to seek His forgiveness and grace.

Perhaps opening a Bible would be a good place to start, if you want to find that Love. The story is told in the very beginning of the New Testament. Matthew 1:18-23 reads: "This is how the birth of Jesus Christ came about ... All this took place to fulfill what the Lord had said through the prophet: "The virgin will be with child and will give birth to a son, and they will call him Immanuel, which means "God with us.""

God, with us. Love, with us - in a room full of the joy of Christmas or in a homeless shelter; in a school room or an office tower; in a hospital or a grocery store; on a bus travelling across the country or a plane taking people home to their loved ones. He is always with us, everywhere. So, this Christmas, take the time to stop opening the presents. Sit back and listen. Love is, indeed, in the room.

A Perfect Choice for The Job

Have you ever wondered, "Why me?" It's usually something we think when things aren't going well, when we feel like we've been singled out for some misfortune. It's a rare thing to think of this question in terms of being chosen for a special honor, being singled out for some blessing.

I wonder if Mary asked herself, "Why me?" After the angel Gabriel was gone, after the startling moment when he announced her destiny, I wonder if she went home and wondered why she of all women was chosen for such an honor?

I imagine the glow from that angel lasted for some time. I imagine it was a long time before Mary was concerned about the negative side of things. Perhaps she never was. Perhaps that's why she was chosen.

Mary was ready to receive whatever God had for her. She didn't try to get out of it, as Moses did when he pleaded with God to choose someone else for the job (Exodus 3:11- 4:13). She didn't ask for another sign, as Gideon did when God called him to fight against a mighty army (Judges 8:36-40). She

Love In The Room

put no conditions on her obedience, as Barak did when God told him He was going to give him victory over his enemy (Judges 4:8). Mary didn't doubt, as Zehariah did when Gabriel appeared to him and told him he would soon have a son (Luke 1:18).

Mary simply agreed to do what God wanted her to do, no matter how impossible or difficult it seemed. "I am the Lord's servant," she said (Luke 1:38).

The angel Garbriel addressed Mary as "you who are highly favored" (Luke 1:28). The Greek word used for highly favored, "charitoo," is used only one other time in the New Testament. It is used in reference to the body of believers, in book of Ephesians, chapter 1, verse 6. The word literally means filled with grace, freely bestowed with all the richness of God - His love, His mercy, His grace and His power.

We, like Mary, are God's perfect choice for the job at hand. How do we respond to such an honour? Are we pleading to God to accomplish His will through someone else, like Moses, or asking for more, like Gideon, or putting conditions on our service, like Barak?

God became one of us, to show us how to respond. He became a man to help us understand that we are highly favored, full of grace. This astounding fact is hard to live with. We are much more inclined to react with fear and doubt. But if we, like Mary, see ourselves in the right perspective, as servants standing in the glow of angels, as men and women not only bowing before the cradle of Christ but in the shadow of the cross, we can and will fulfill our destiny.

And then, like Mary, we will say, "My soul praises the Lord and my spirit rejoices in God my Savior" (Luke 1: 46-47).

Love In The Room

No Matter What

About this time every year someone comes up to me and starts talking about the pagan traditions of Christmas. The tradition of a Christmas tree, for instance, is said to have originated with the pagan practice of bringing evergreen boughs, or a "Yule Tree" into the home as a symbol of the new life that would come after the winter.

People also complain that the 25th of December has nothing at all to do with the birth of Jesus. Historians believe He was likely born in the springtime. Some scholars maintain that December 25th was only adopted in the 4th Century as a Christian holiday by the Roman Emperor Constantine, to encourage a common religious festival for both Christians and pagans. Historical documents do not seem to bear this out, however. There is no actual evidence, beyond assumptions, that the holiday was actually instituted by the Emperor. In fact most evidence indicates that it was adopted decades after his death in most parts of the Empire.

Another thing that usually crops up at Christmas is the use of Xmas. Many Christians take offense to this, feeling it somehow denigrates the name of Christ. The word *Christmas* is a contraction of *Christ's Mass*, derived from the Old English *Cristes mæsse* and referring to the religious ceremony of the Catholic mass. The abbreviation *Xmas* probably came about because the English letter X resembles the Greek letter Χ (chi), the first letter of *Christ* in Greek (Χριστός transliterated as [Christos]). Xmas is pronounced the same as Christmas, but most people just say X-Mas.

Whether or not you know and believe this information, the celebration of Christmas is now, and forevermore will be, a Christian event. These days there is a movement afoot to get rid of the traditional holiday names and greetings all together. "Merry Christmas" has been amended to "Happy Holidays," nativity scenes are banned from many public places and more and more secular music is taking the place of the long-sung carols.

But none of this can change the fact that Christ is at the core of Christmas. It was the Christ child who was born to save the world, the Christ man who lived among us and taught us about His Father, the Christ God who died on that cross over two thousand years ago, to accomplish His Father's will. No speculations about origins, no attempt to secularize the traditions will change that reality.

Whether or not you know and believe in the Christ, He was born in a stable in Palestine, He did

Love In The Room

walk the earth performing miracle after miracle, He was tried by Pontius Pilate, was crucified, died and was buried.

Whether or not you believe he was God, He was raised from the dead by his Father after three days and because of Him all of us have access to God and the hope of eternal life.

That's the story of Christmas. That's reason to celebrate, no matter what.

Can Anything Good Come …?

The young girl before us shone with a light that came from inside of her. She spoke joyfully about a day, just a few weeks before, when God touched her body and healed her. Then she spoke even more simply, of how God touched her soul and healed it too. The girl was from Ukarumpa, a small village in Papua New Guinea - a village known for its violence and lawlessness. As we left the church that morning, I heard someone remark that he had been deeply humbled by what he'd heard that morning. "I never thought I'd see anything good come from Ukarumpa," he said.

A similar comment was made long ago about a small town in the area known then as Palestine. A man named Philip had met Jesus and immediately ran to tell his brother, Nathanael. "Philip found Nathanael and said to him, "We have found Him of whom Moses in the Law and also the Prophets wrote --Jesus of Nazareth, the son of Joseph." (John 1:45) I imagine Nathanael laughed and mocked his brother as he said, "Can any good thing come out of Nazareth?" (v.46). The town was known to be less than prosperous, less than acceptable in the eyes of those in larger towns and cities like Jerusalem. Yet

Love In The Room

that is where the Son of God resided for most of his life on earth. He was born and lived in humble estate.

All of us can take comfort in that fact. We don't have to be anything special, or have come from high-class wealthy families, to be precious to God. He demonstrated his love for all when he came, not dressed in the robes of royalty, but with a carpenter's hammer in His hand.

We can take comfort too, in knowing that the healing that young girl in Papua New Guinea experienced is available to all of us, no matter where we're from or where we've been, no matter where we started out, or what we've become. God does not reserve His mercy and love for those who think their lives are perfect. He pours it out on those who are destitute and spiritually blind, those who have failed and those who are living in darkness. The truth is, we are all in that state spiritually, whether we were born into poverty or riches. All of us are born into places like Nazareth and Ukarumpa, into an inheritance of violence and death. That's why Jesus was born and why he died. His death paid the price we could never afford. The girl in Papua New Guinea shone with the love of Christ because she had accepted God's love and forgiveness. That simple act will make us all whole.

Something good did happen in Ukarumpa. And our Saviour did come from Nazareth.

It's That Time of Year

It's that time again, the time when people begin to turn their minds and energies toward Christmas. Churches are preparing their pageants, banquets and special events. Christmas parties are being arranged and people are out looking for those special gifts to send to friends and family. Shopkeepers decorate to attract gift seekers and carols can be heard in almost every place of business. There seems to be a general bustle about town as the banners and tinsel go up on lampposts and doorframes. Everyone, it seems, is trying to get into the spirit of the season.

But not everyone, it seems, succeeds. For some the Christmas season is drudgery. It's a time when they have to work harder but don't get paid any more, a time when all the decorations and glittering shop windows are just reminders of what they can't have. For some, Christmas is a time of unbearable pain and stress as they face a first, or yet another, holiday without their life's companion or loved one. For some, Christmas means facing the reality that relationships are broken and may never be restored.

Love In The Room

The irony is that Jesus came for those people, those who are too despondent to care. He came for those who are poor and downtrodden, those who are suffering and in emotional pain. He came for those who need, not tinsel and decorations, but a solid rock to hold on to. The other irony is that those who focus on all the trappings of Christmas may be those who are even more desperately in need, but don't know it. They see only the superficiality of the season, the parties and the gifts, without understanding there is only one gift worth the celebration – Jesus Himself.

Whatever camp you find yourself in, the great hope of Christmas is that Jesus came for all of us. His mission was to reveal the glory of His Father to a world that had long been unable to see it. His mission today is the same. Whether you are a shopper with a healthy bank account, or a beggar with none, Jesus has a message for you – "the Son of Man came to seek and to save what was lost" (Luke 19:10).

So, let's rejoice in the season, not for its glitter and tinsel but for the glory of God revealed in the birth of a baby, not for its music and parties but for the love of a Saviour. With every carol we hear, let's praise Him. With every gift we wrap, let's thank Him. With every garland we string, let's give glory to God. It's that time of year.

Pretty Packages

My co-worker slipped a brightly-wrapped package onto the desk near the computer where I was working. "This is for you," she said quietly, smiled and walked away. Having delivered a small package myself, earlier in the day, I was pleased. This "Kris Kringle" gift exchange was working just as it should. I glanced at my present. The wrapping was colourful, ringed with red ribbon and a small wreath of glistening holly that circled the tag with my name on it. It was too pretty to open right away, so I set it aside until the end of my shift.

Finally one of my other co-workers said, "Well? Aren't you going to open it? How can you let it just sit there?"

In my own defense, I explained that it was so pretty I just wanted to admire it. When I finally did open it, as carefully as possible, I was pleased with the contents. In fact, once I saw what was inside, I forgot all about the wrapping. The gift, of course, was far more valuable than the paper and ribbon. It is a gift I can use, one that will bring pleasure for some time.

Often we look at aspects of living a 'good' life in

Love In The Room

the same way I looked at my 'Kris Kringle' present. Principles like forgiveness, truth, love and kindness look good. We all admire them. We nod our heads with assent when they are discussed. We even acknowledge they would be good to incorporate into our lives. But too often these principles remain unwrapped. They sometimes stay that way for a very long time. We continue to admire them, but we never make them part of our daily experience. We don't unwrap and use them. As good as they may appear, they are useless until we do.

Forgiveness, truth, love and kindness. They are only pretty packages unless we put them to use. Unwrapping them means we must put a small pronoun and an active verb in front of the words: I will forgive; I will speak the truth; I will love, I will be kind. There is a wonderful bonus to using these principles actively in our lives. Unlike Christmas gifts, once they are opened they are never used up, because they are never kept to ourselves.

Forgiveness, truth, love, and kindness, when they become realities in our lives, change us and the lives of those around us. The lives of those around them are changed. These are gifts that go on giving. Forgiveness, truth, love and kindness are gifts that can change your world. James 1:22 says, "Do not merely listen to the word … Do what it says. Or, in the words of my friend – "Aren't you going to open it? How can you let it just sit there?"

Artificial Light

Psalm 19:1 says – "The heavens declare the glory of God; the skies proclaim the work of his hands. Day after day they pour fourth speech; night after night they display knowledge."

I now take those words literally since watching a video called The Star of Bethlehem (produced by Stephen McEveety, presented by Rick Larson). It is astounding how God orchestrated even the movement of the stars and planets to tell us that his son, our Messiah, was being born.

Unfortunately, we have obscured the message. If we look up at all, we rarely see the heavens as the glory of God. We have forgotten to look for the signs he has left us; we have neglected the knowledge displayed for our understanding. The lights and smog from our cities dim the brilliance of the skies, just as the noise and frantic pace of our lives replaces the peace and joy that should characterize the Christmas season.

We have created artificial light to fill our homes and streets, thinking it gives us the light we need. Even the decorative lights nailed to the outside of our homes to signal that the Christmas season has begun, seem to point us only to what can be bought

Love In The Room

from the malls. To most, they signal the buying season, not the Messiah's redemption.

Yet there is hope. Every now and then someone looks to the skies and wonders. Every now and then someone stops in the middle of the mall and ponders. Every now and then, someone smiles at a crèche in a public place and whispers a thank you. And in between A Holly Jolly Christmas, and Jingle Bell Rock, we do still hear the sweetness of Away in a Manger.

No matter how much artificial light we produce, His light cannot be dimmed. His flame will never be extinguished. And His purposes will move forward to the very end of the age. He put the stars in place and the planets in their orbits. He sent His son to die for us all and one day He will send Him back again to bring it all to its final conclusion.

Perhaps, this Christmas, when we put that plastic star on the top of our artificial Christmas tree it would be well to remember that there was a real star of Bethlehem that heralded the most significant moment in the history of mankind – the birth of our Messiah.

Enough

It was a small cast of characters, but it was enough. There was an ordinary man, a carpenter, forced to take his pregnant wife on a long journey just when she was about to give birth. The imposed census had made refugees out of everyone in their country. The small town overflowed with weary travellers. Their accommodations that night were rough but the heat from the animals would be enough to keep them warm.

There were the shepherds, hunkered down in the fields, their bleating sheep around them. Perhaps they had a small fire going - enough to keep the chill of the night at bay. And then there was that angel. Just one, but it was enough to make those shepherds shake with fear until he told them why he was there – to tell them "tidings of great joy." And then, just to emphasize the point, a "great company of the heavenly host appeared with the angel, praising God ..." (Luke 2:13). That was enough to make those shepherds want to find out if what the angel had told them was really true. It was easy to find the place – the light of that unusually bright star was enough.

It was enough, too, for those rich men who came, later. Rich men, they were, with enough resources

Love In The Room

to give expensive gifts to a small baby found in very humble circumstances. Perhaps they wondered if they really should, but seeing that star stop in that exact place was enough of a sign for them. They laid the gifts by the manger and worshiped the tiny king. The expensive gifts would be enough to carry him and his family to safety in Egypt.

Yes, it was a small cast of characters playing out the greatest drama ever known to mankind that clear night in Bethlehem. Did they know He would be enough? Did they know that His birth would become so renowned it would be enough for men to make it the pivot of history? Did they know that when he had grown into a man just a touch from his hands would be enough to make blind men see? Did they know that the words from His mouth would be enough to calm a raging sea and raise the dead? Did they understand that He was the One whose death would be enough to wipe their sins away, enough to cause the gates of heaven to open and the curtain to the holy of holies ripped in two?

Perhaps they did not completely understand, but the light of the world had come and yes, those men would learn, as millions more beyond them through the centuries, that Jesus is enough. "For to us a child is born, to us a son is given … And he will be called Wonderful Counselor, Mighty God, Everlasting Father, Prince of Peace. (Isaiah 9:6).

Rejoicing in the Present

It's almost the end of November, we have lots of snow on the ground and the temperatures are telling us it's definitely winter. Some of my neighbours turned on their Christmas lights this week and a friend emailed to say she had put her tree up. We're planning the Christmas program and dinner at our church and we've even started to sing the carols.

It all makes me smile. It's a little early for me to turn the outdoor lights on or put the tree up, but I am looking forward to Christmas. Looking forward to the bright decorations, to having my family around a table laden with good food, to the laughter and perhaps even tears as we open our presents.

Traditionally Christmas is a time to look back, far back, to a day over two thousand years ago, when a tiny baby was born in a village in the Middle East. But, because of who that child was, it is also a time to look forward and a time to ponder the present. That child, Jesus Christ, was God's present to us, a child who was to change the course of future history, not just for a space of time on this earth, but eternally in that mysterious place called heaven.

Love In The Room

Because of Jesus, heaven would be populated with humanity, those who would accept Him as their Saviour and the Son of God.

But I'm also trying to practise the 'present' of Christmas in another way – taking time to pause and enjoy all the moments, all that comes with this season – the music that tells the story in public places, the lights that proclaim His glory on the streets, the bustle of shoppers on a city street that speak of the spirit of giving and grace.

I'm also practising the 'present' of Christmas by taking time to pause and listen for the Saviour's voice, time to read His story from the Bible and get to know Him more. I know my present – every moment of the day - can be transcendent when I draw close to Him. I rejoice in each day He gives me, enjoying His creation, yes, even the snow and cold temperatures, His people, family, friends, even strangers, and most of all, His presence.

This Christmas I'll be looking back, looking forward and rejoicing in the present. All because of Jesus.

Beginnings and Endings

I was shopping yesterday, picking up the last of the items on my list for Christmas. I told the woman at the counter I was finished. "That's it," I said. "I'm done." Then my cell phone rang. It was my daughter, asking to be picked up from school. As I drove, I mentally went down the girls' wish lists and I realized I'd forgotten something. Laura still had some shopping to do too, so we went back to the same store. (The 50% off sign is a big draw in our family!)

The clerk smiled pleasantly. "I thought you were done."

I grinned and nodded. "So did I."

It seems we're never done. There's always another gift to get, another item to buy for the Christmas dinner, another invitation to give out for that party before the 25th. Then, all of a sudden, it's over. The day is past, the gifts are put away, the tree is tossed out. Then the plans begin for New Year's – more invitations to give and receive, more food to buy. We're never done.

I imagine Mary, like most women who give birth, breathed a deep sigh of relief when Jesus was born. After the long nine-month wait, at last it was

Love In The Room

finished. But the birth of Christ, as no other, was not an end but a beginning. It was a new beginning for us all, a new agreement between man and God. It took thirty-some years to bring the plan into fulfillment, but there was no doubt it would come to be. The end was in sight from the moment of Christ's birth. He was the baby who came to die, and His death, like His birth, was like no other.

When Jesus said, "It is finished," (John 19:30), He wasn't referring to just the span of thirty years he spent on earth. He was referring to the plan set in motion from eternity past – the plan to bring all of mankind into right relationship with God. His part was done, once and for all, as He took the sin of mankind on Himself and removed the barrier between human beings and God. His part was done, but our part was just beginning.

The birth and death of Jesus gave us all the chance to say yes to Him, to discover and develop a relationship with Him, and to tell others about Him. His birth gave us all life, His death gave us all forgiveness, and His resurrection gave us all purpose. When we accept that, we will never be done, neither in growing like Him, nor in receiving and dispensing His love. It's going to go on forever.

That's a reason to celebrate! So let the carols ring and the feasting never end. "For to us a child is born, to us a son is given…And he will be called Wonderful Counselor, Mighty God, Everlasting Father, Prince of Peace (Isaiah 9:6).

Letting Go

"What room can I de-clutter now?" My daughter grinned at me. I didn't grin back. "Slow down," I said, "we have six months before we move." She laughed and said it might take longer to do the down-sizing we will have to do to move from a five bedroom into a two-bedroom house. It isn't going to be easy for me. I confess I am a packrat and I tend to hold on to things a little too tightly. Things like books. My other daughter said we should advertise this way – "House For Sale, Includes Library." I didn't grin at that comment, either.

The problem is that so many of the things around me have a story attached. Many of the things are connected to people – friends and family. Letting them go means letting go of emotional attachments and memories, so it's hard, even though I tell myself that those friends are still there and the family memories will always remain in my mind. I like having tangible reminders, things I can see and hold. I am comfortable in the midst of my clutter. Perhaps I have security issues, but the thought of leaving it all is a little frightening.

I can't imagine what it must have been like for the Son of God to leave his home in heaven. He was in a

Love In The Room

position of exaltation – a place of power and honour and glory. Yet He stepped away from it all to be born in a humble place in the middle of a dark world. He would know all the pain and sorrow of that world as he grew, and then that world, the very people for whom he had given up so much, would turn against him and crucify him.

Knowing all of that, He still came to us, still gave up all that he had known, for the love of a people who would reject Him.

Jesus had no security issues. He knew exactly who He was and who His Father was. He knew the plan, the glorious plan laid out for mankind and He was willing to do His part to accomplish it.

It is fitting, therefore, that we celebrate Christmas. It is fitting that children dress up in bathrobes and mimic ancient costumes to help us remember. It is fitting that choirs sing about wise men who traveled great distances to meet him, that ordinary common people bow their knee before his manger. There has been no greater sacrifice. There has been no greater love. There will never be a greater Saviour than the one who came as a tiny baby some two thousand years ago.

"Glory to God in the highest, and on earth peace to men on whom his favor rests" (Luke 2:14).

How do You Picture The Christ of Christmas?

Have you made your Christmas list yet? I watched my daughter do hers the other day. The first few items seemed to come easily but she had to think hard to figure out what else to add. Eventually she handed it to me and made sure I understood the details about each item. We all have our wish lists, things we'd like to see under the Christmas tree.

We all have another kind of list too. Sometimes the list is long and all about selfish desires; wants instead of needs. These are the things we pray about. We may find a way to make our requests seem righteous, but scratch the surface and they're really all about "me." We see God as a Santa Claus. He's only there to give us what we want and make life go a little easier.

Sometimes we see God as The Grinch. He's the one who's just waiting to spoil all the fun, the one who hates to hear us laugh and sing, the one who judges and condemns. He really doesn't want anything to do with us. He'd prefer to stay aloof, but sometimes he just can't resist the urge to mess things up. He's The Grinch who lives in a high place and nobody in his or her right mind would want to approach him.

Love In The Room

There's a third picture of God, one we see on Christmas cards. It's a picture of a tiny baby held in his mother's arms or laying on a bed of straw. He looks pretty helpless, as helpless as any newborn. There's not much point in praying to him.

Each one of these pictures of God is flawed. God is not a Santa. He isn't always going to give us what we ask for. He knows that what we ask for isn't always in our best interest, nor the best interests of others. He isn't a Grinch. He loves to hear us laugh and sing, especially when we are delighting in Him. Neither is He an impotent little baby. He's the master of the universe, the one who put the stars in the sky and set the planets in their orbits.

The Christ of Christmas is approachable, loving, wise and all-powerful. But you will never see Him that way if all you do is beg him for presents as though He were Santa, fear his condemnation as though He were the Grinch, or blind yourself to his power as though he were just a tiny baby. If you desire to see Christ as He really is, ask Him to reveal Himself to you. That is the one request He will never refuse. His Spirit will open your eyes and heart, and "then you will know the truth, and the truth will set you free" (John 8:32). Pick up a Bible and seek Him. Ask the Holy Spirit to reveal Him and you will find the true Christ of Christmas.

Too Much Christmas

"I baked a bit." My mother-in-law smiled as my husband piled the tins of cookies, Christmas cakes, chocolates and tarts on the counter. "I should say you did!" He said and we all chuckled.

Then Christmas day came and the turkey and mashed potatoes and stuffing and cranberry sauce and pumpkin pies. We ate the left-overs for weeks. I think I gained at five pounds through that season. By the time my mother-in-law left we were all feeling like we'd had a little too much Christmas. One of my daughters commented that maybe it would be a good idea to scale things down a notch the next year.

In our prosperous North American society, it's easy to take things to an excess that is neither of spiritual benefit nor physically healthy. All the gift giving and trappings of Christmas are good to a point, but when things go overboard the true significance of the season can easily be buried under all the celebration. We get excited about the decorating and baking and gift buying and forget that our Saviour was born in a rough stable with no glitz, no glitter and most likely the most basic food.

Love In The Room

Those who knew His true identity came in secret to pay homage. Even the angels were restricted in their announcement, appearing to the most humble of that society, shepherds tending their flocks. That first Christmas day was the most significant time in history, yet it was wrapped, not in loud fanfare and celebration, but in a quiet awe and reverence.

We are a little like the apostle Peter after he witnessed one of the most astounding events of Christ's time on the earth – His transfiguration. Seeing Elijah and Moses speaking with Jesus, Peter exclaims – "I will put up three shelters…" (Matthew 17:4). His first inclination was to celebrate but he had no idea what he was saying, no idea that he was in fact bringing Jesus down to the same level as the two prophets of old. God the Father does not waste any time correcting him. "While he was still speaking, a bright cloud covered them, and a voice from the cloud said, "This is my Son, whom I love; with him I am well pleased. Listen to him!" (Matthew 17:5). The father dismissed Peter's plan to surround the event with "trappings" and made it clear what they should do instead. It was a rather straight-forward command – "Listen to him!"

Perhaps we should remember that moment as we celebrate Christmas, remember to look beyond all the trappings of the season and acknowledge the One who was born to give His life for us. Perhaps we should all scale things down a notch. Instead of too much "Christmas" perhaps we should focus on listening for the voice of the Christ.

Wishing I Could be Jesus

I recently attended a funeral for a young man who died too soon, leaving a wife and three young girls. The sadness overwhelms at times and it makes me wish I could be Jesus, just for a few minutes, just long enough to say, as He did, "arise."

But then, I realize that He doesn't need me to do His work for Him. He has already done it. He has already said that wondrous, mysterious word and brought that young man into His kingdom, given him time to have a productive, full life here on this earth, and then brought Him home, to the place where he has wanted to be, as a believer in Christ.

Often things don't seem right to us. The world seems off kilter and full of so much pain and suffering it overwhelms. And we want to be Jesus. We want to snap our fingers and make it all better. But He has already been at work. He has a plan for this earth, a plan that goes far beyond what we could ever imagine. He told the Hebrew people that when they were in circumstances that were full of pain and suffering – their captivity in Babylon. Living as slaves, they no doubt often cried out to God to bring them relief from all the suffering and pain they saw around them.

Love In The Room

This was His answer – "For I know the plans I have for you," declares the Lord, "Plans to prosper you and not to harm you, plans to give you hope and a future. Then you will call on me and come and I will listen to you. You will seek me and find me when you seek me with all your heart" (Jeremiah 29:11-13).

At this time of year some of us are in circumstances that are made even more difficult by all the joy and/or jollity around us. And sadness overwhelms.

Here are a few things we can do when that happens:

Look up. When we see all those decorated Christmas trees, look up. Look for the star or the angel on the top. And know Jesus is with you.

Look around. There are others who are struggling. Is there something you can do for them that will lighten their hearts, and yours?

Look ahead. Jesus has promised a bright future, and given us a way to know we are secure in his hand.

Yes, there are times I wish I could be Jesus. But then I remember – He is the Messiah, the Living God, our hope and our comfort. We don't need anything else.

The Only Gift We Need

Normally at this time of year I'm running from shop to shop with thousands of others, searching for just the right gifts for family and friends. This year, though my chemotherapy treatments are finally over, I just don't have the energy yet to do it.

I've made a couple of forays into the stores but haven't gotten very far before I need to rest. I'm afraid the stockings won't be as full this year, but it's with a thankful heart that I realize it doesn't really matter.

I know my family and friends will still love me, even if their stockings aren't bulging. I know it because over the past few months they have shown it. I have been overwhelmed with the outpouring of love and support from so many who have told me they are praying, brought meals, sent cards and even gifts, or just dropped by for a visit.

All of them have shown me the face of Jesus in these things. They have shown me a tiny slice of His character, by doing what He would do, love unconditionally. It's an astounding thing to recognize in friends and family and most especially in God. We know He knows us better than anyone; He knows us inside and out, yet He still loves us so

Love In The Room

much He was willing to humble himself, be born in a stable and then die on a cross to ensure that we have the opportunity to be reconciled to Him and to live with Him forever. Amazing!

Normally, at this time of year, I'd be running with the crowds. It's kind of nice not to be. It's kind of awe inspiring to slow down and ponder the amazing love of family, friends, and most especially, Jesus. It's kind of what Christmas should be all about - the reason for the season - the unconditional, amazing, awe-inspiring love of Jesus.

It's the only gift any of us needs.

Thoughts on Christmas Kitsch

I sat at the table for five hours, watching people walk by. Every now and then someone would stop and pick up one of my books. I'd chat with them, telling them the book was a collection of devotionals. Sometimes I'd share how the Lord had used it to make a change in someone's life. Usually they'd smile and move on. They'd move on to buy trinkets at other tables loaded with kitsch – painted plastic santas, neon snowflakes, angels made of dishtowels, and snowmen made of styrofoam.

As the day wore on I got a little discouraged. And, as discouragement often does, it started to move into bitterness tinged with anger. Why were these people so eager to grab things that had so little value and would last for such a short time? Why weren't they more interested in buying something that could nourish their souls? It made me want to scream, but I kept quiet and tried to keep smiling when someone glanced my way.

As I drove home later that day I ruminated. I love that word – it means to turn over and over, as in a cow chewing her cud. And that's what it felt like as I drove along – my stomach was churning; I was stewing and I wasn't being very complimentary to

Love In The Room

those people who had not bought my books.

Then that still small voice whispered from somewhere beyond – "And what about you?"

"Me, Lord? Um … What do you mean?"

I didn't really have to ask. I knew what He meant. I too make choices every day, choices that are just like those kitsch-hunters. I choose things that are of little value and momentary pleasure over the riches and everlasting joys of Christ. Every day. I was humbled there in my car, and had to do an attitude adjustment. I had to ask God to forgive me for my "holier than thou" thoughts. I had to thank Him for those who did buy my books and thank Him for what he was going to do in their lives through my mere words. And I had to ask Him to forgive me for all those times I've chosen the kitsch of the world over Him.

The verses in Deuteronomy filled my mind - "Now choose life, so that you and your children may live and you may love the Lord your God, listen to his voice and hold fast to him. For the Lord is your life…" (Deut.30:19-20).

There's an awful lot of kitsch in this world, especially at this time of year. It's tempting to allow ourselves to be distracted from the real story of Christmas. As the season unfolds, may we all avoid running after what cannot satisfy. May we all choose life.

The Promise of Christmas

Chaos reigned supreme. That's how it seemed as we rehearsed our Christmas play. The first rehearsal didn't really happen. The second one was only a bit better, and three quarters of the cast didn't make it to the third. Those of us who were supposedly in control worried that it would never work.

That was nothing new. Every year it seems to happen. Kids run helter-skelter, some don't show up, some can't find costumes or those made for them don't fit. The choir director is tearing her hair out This year seemed a bit more chaotic than usual. But somehow it all came together in the end. The night of the performance seemed to go well. I say seemed, because I was too busy trying to keep my "cast" quiet and focused, to notice if the play was working. One of the magi discovered he could use one of the shepherd's headbands as a slingshot to wing the beads off his crown clear across the front of the church. That delighted the kids in the front row who dashed out to pick them up. Mary couldn't stop squirming because her costume was made of wool, and Joseph kept changing his mind about which robe fit best – right up until he walked out onto the 'stage.'

Love In The Room

I wasn't sure it had really all come together until the audience stood to applaud at the end. When many congratulated us on a job well done, all I could say was, "It's a miracle!"

And that's the promise of Christmas – it all comes together in the end. I'm sure the followers of Jesus, watching the drama of His life and death, felt the same way we 'directors' did. To those who thought they were in control, it looked like chaos reigned. From the moment of His birth, He and His parents had to run from those who wanted to kill Him. As He performed miracles, religious leaders plotted against Him. Even the disciples themselves didn't understand His message. They were disappointed that He didn't chase the Romans out of the country; He never did set up an earthly kingdom. Then, the cross. It looked like everything they tried to accomplish was doomed to fail. But in the end ...

In the end, the stone was rolled away. The baby born in a stable and crucified on a cross was raised glorified, to the glory of His Father.

And there is another promise yet to unfold. As the birth of Christ is overshadowed by the cross, which was blasted away by his resurrection, even that will be outdone by His return. One day, God has told us, "Before me every knee will bow; by me every tongue will swear. They will say of me, 'In the Lord alone are righteousness and strength'" (Isaiah 45:23,24). It will be a miracle and it really will all come together in the end.

God's Gifts are Not For You

"Did you have a good Christmas? What did you get?"

Those two sentences seem to go hand in hand. I've heard them several times in the past week, as people chatted with my kids. The girls always gave the same answer, naming a couple of their favorite gifts. As I listened to the exchange, I chuckled to myself. There were a couple of presents given this year that were not really intended for the recipient. One of the girls gave 'the family' a large perfumed candle. "To go in the bathroom," she said, grinning. The rest of us grinned back - we all know who spends hours in the tub.

You've probably been given one or two gifts of that sort at some point, if not at Christmas, perhaps for your birthday. Many wives have received such 'useful' presents - a set of pots and pans; a blender; an iron. I remember one my husband gave me many years ago. We were building a house at the time so I suppose it was a practical gift, but a shiny new Spalding saw was not what I had envisioned for my birthday! He grinned a lot when he gave it to me, like my daughter did when we unwrapped that candle. We both knew who was going to do the sawing.

Love In The Room

Like that candle and that saw, God's gifts are not just intended for the recipient. He intends to use them Himself. It is up to us to put hands and feet to those intentions by serving others. The prophet Isaiah new this when he said, "The Sovereign Lord has given me an instructed tongue, to know the word that sustains the weary." (Isaiah 50:4) The writer of 1 Corinthians also knew the principle well. He stresses that the gifts God gives are intended, not for the benefit or honor of those employing them, but for the "strengthening of the church." (1Cor.14:26) The apostle Peter makes this clear when he says - "Each one should use whatever gift he has received to serve others, faithfully administering God's grace in its various forms" (1 Peter 4:10).

God's gifts are intended for others, but we also benefit when we use what we have been given, both spiritual gifts and natural talents, to that end. There is no greater sense of satisfaction than that which comes when we have used what we have been given to strengthen others. Whether it is in providing a meal on Christmas day for those in need, teaching Mathematics in grade 2, providing efficient secretarial skills in an office, digging a ditch for a sewer line or a post hole for a fence to keep the cows in, or preaching a sermon on Sunday morning; if you are using the gifts God gave you, you will be blessed.

So. Did you have a good Christmas? What did you get?

Window Shopping

The street twinkled with Christmas lights. Our boots crunched on a skiff of snow that had fallen the night before and my daughters and I smiled and laughed as we window shopped, chatting about possible gifts for members of our family. It was fun window shopping – oohing and ahhing over the bright Christmas displays and pointing out things we liked. Now and then we'd see something we all thought was particularly ugly and we'd all groan at the same time. Now and then the display in the window was enough to draw us into the store.

Window shopping is fun, but it can't beat being able to walk into the store and buy the perfect gift. It can't beat taking it home and wrapping it in bright paper, knowing it will soon make your loved one's eyes light up when they open it. It can't beat the feeling of anticipation as you put it under the tree.

As we turn to spiritual things during the Christmas season, too often many of us just window shop. On the internet, it's called lurking. We look but don't buy, we listen but don't participate. Standing on the outside looking in has its advantages. We believe it's a safe place – God can't ask anything of us if we don't make a commitment. We won't have to change if we stay on the edge and stay quiet.

Love In The Room

But window shoppers never get to feel the excitement of finding the perfect gift. Lurkers never get to express their feelings and thoughts – no relationship develops with other people of like mind. Similarly, those who do not make a commitment to Christ never know the joy of the gift of salvation. They are never able to dialogue with Jesus as a friend, a brother, a saviour. Too many are missing the perfect gift – the gift of Jesus himself.

Are you window shopping but never buying? Are you lurking but never participating? Find the true joy of Christmas this year. Step inside where it's warm. Find that perfect gift and take it home. The perfect gift is Jesus Christ and He's waiting for you.

"For to us a child is born, to us a son is given, and the government will be on his shoulders. And he will be called Wonderful Counselor, Mighty God, Everlasting Father, Prince of Peace" (Isaiah 9:6).

A Baby in a Box

I'm a push-over when it comes to babies. I'm not the type to coo at every one I see, but I can't look at a baby without feeling my heart go soft. I guess that's why I love T.V. commercials with babies in them, even though I realize the advertisers are trying to manipulate me. There's been a cute one on lately. It shows a little one in diapers playing in an empty box. The audio specifies the cost of toys and other things purchased online. Then the voice says, 'The cost of watching her play with the empty box instead? Priceless.' Anyone who has watched a toddler at Christmas knows the truth of that statement. It's a good illustration of the cliche, "money can't buy everything."

Most of us know the valuable things in life cannot be bought; things like peace, fulfillment, happiness and love. We know it, but do we believe it? It's said that we all have preferred values and real values; what you truly believe is evidenced by what you do. If a man says he cares about his family but spends all his time at work, his real value is work. If a woman says she loves her husband but has a string of affairs, her real value is herself. If a person says he values the simple life, but spends time and string of affairs, her real value is herself. If a person

Love In The Room

money accumulating 'stuff,' his real value is material possessions. If someone says she treasures the Word of God but rarely reads it, her true value is in other pursuits.

It's easy to let our preferred values take a back seat. Distractions and temptations abound and our nature does not lend itself easily to doing what is right. Even the apostle Paul had this problem. He admits he does what he does not want to do: "So I find this law at work: when I want to do good, evil is right there with me. For in my inner being I delight in God's law; but I see another law at work in the members of my body, waging war against the law of my mind and making me a prisoner of the law of sin...What a wretched man I am!" (Romans 7:21-24).

Paul's dilemma is universal. We would love to be like that little baby on T.V., happy and content with little, but we find ourselves distracted and tempted until we are trapped in a complex world of our own making, doing all the things we do not want to do. Paul's solution is also universal. He says - "Who will rescue me from this body of death? Thanks be to God - through Christ Jesus our Lord!" Knowing that Christ is the answer takes the sting out of the problem. Preferred values can become real values. We can do what is right, through Jesus Christ.

As the New Year approaches, there could be no better resolution than to become like that little child and joyfully follow Him.

The Week After

The week after Christmas always seems a bit like the twilight zone to me. The fuss and flurry of Christmas is over but the New Year is still a few days away and everything seems to be on hold. That's why it's the perfect time for pondering.

I was straightening up around the Christmas tree this week, and looked up just as the sun dipped. The angel on my windowsill became a silhouette while the three hand-made carollers beside it seemed to glow. I love my angel - I love that he's extremely tall, which is an accurate depiction according to the Bible. I love his copper wings and long crimson gown. I love the serenity on his face. I also have a particular fondness for my little carolers, even though they're made of Styrofoam and cloth and I usually have to reattach their heads at least once during the season. As I looked at them that day it seemed that the tall one was looking down and protecting the small ones. It made me smile.

As I pondered them that day, I thought of all the times I've lived so totally in this world without any sense or understanding that there is another realm watching. I do believe in angels. I've known people who swear they've been visited by them, helped in

Love In The Room

some way. Perhaps my positioning of my angel beside and slightly behind my carollers was a subconscious nod in that direction. But I don't think about angels very often.

The Bible tells us that angels are "ministering spirits sent to serve those who will inherit salvation" (Hebrews 1:14). Their appearances in the Bible tell us they refused to be worshiped and always pointed to the One who sent them. I'm quite sure there are many times that angels help us in some way and we remain unaware.

Just look at the famous story in the Bible about Elisha and his servant. When the servant despaired because they were surrounded by their enemies, Elisha asked God to show him what was really there and "he looked and saw the hills full of horses and chariots of fire all around Elisha" (2Kings 6:17).

As I looked at my tall angel and my little carollers that day I wondered about all the angels who watch over us and God's goodness in providing them. There are times when I wish I could see them, as Elisha's servant did, but I don't have to see them to know they are there. God has promised to keep us under his wing, protected. He has promised to guide us with his Spirit. He has promised He will never leave us.

These are fine promises to take with us into the New Year. Whatever it may hold for us, we can know God is with us. His angels are hovering near. May He bless you all abundantly with all the spiritual riches of His mercy and grace.

To Resolve or not To Resolve

I was delivering Christmas cards last week and stopped in to the small gym where, lately, I have been noticeable only by my absence. I admit I felt a little guilty going in the door. The owner greeted me with a wide smile and we wished one another a Merry Christmas. Then I said, "One of my New Year's resolutions will be to get here more often."

My friend shook her head. "Oh don't do that, don't make yourself feel guilty about it!" Then she stammered a bit. "But .... I don't mean .... Do come back!"

We laughed and I assured her I would.

I've been thinking about what she said ever since. I've been thinking about guilt. It does seem to be a big part of what we do at this time of year. We feel guilty for all the things we didn't do in the past year and most of us resolve to do better. So guilt isn't such a bad thing, if, and that's a big if, we make the changes necessary in our lives. If guilt is unresolved it becomes an unhealthy thing and can lead to bitterness and anger that will only make us miserable. But guilt that leads to change, that's healthy guilt.

Love In The Room

So, I have decided to make that New Year's resolution, and a few others, and I've gone a step further. I have a plan for carrying it out. Often that's the key. If we just dwell on our guilty feelings and set no goals or plans for how to change, nothing constructive will happen. Unhealthy guilt will result.

I've heard many people scoff and say that all religion does is make you feel guilty. They are absolutely right. But Jesus has gone a step further. He has set out a plan that wipes away the guilt. All we have to do is move from religion to relationship. When we accept Him as our brother, our friend, our saviour, no amount of guilt can hold us down.

The word guilt appears a few times in the Bible. My favourite is in the book of Hebrews, chapter 10, verse 22 – "let us draw near to God with a sincere heart in full assurance of faith, having our hearts sprinkled to cleanse us from a guilty conscience and having our bodies washed with pure water."
I like those words, "assurance", "cleanse" and "washed with pure water." Though the guilt of our sin may bear us down, there is forgiveness. No matter what we have done, or what has been done to us, God forgives, and we are set free "by a new and living way opened for us through the curtain, that is, his body..." (Hebrews 10:20).

The best resolution any of us can make as we move into the new year is to get to know Him more. I pray we will all resolve to do so. It's the only way to get rid of all that guilt.

Future Tense

2018. It seems like future time. Wasn't it just yesterday that 1984 was so far away we thought we'd never get there? Then came 2000, a new millennium. And on we go. The years race after one another as though they are competing in the Indy 500. And I can't keep up. Maybe I'm feeling my age. The big 65 is looming and I just can't wrap my head around the idea.

But then I read a verse like "Whoever believes in the Son has eternal life…" John 3:36, and John 3:16 – "For God so loved the world that he gave his one and only Son, that whoever believes in him shall not perish but have eternal life." And I am encouraged. Eternal life. I can't wrap my mind around that concept, either, but I know it's a promise I can count on, because my God is faithful and merciful beyond knowing.

And I know it's not going to be a boring life. It's going to be so full we'll have to be glorified to contain it. Wow. Now that's a concept! Glorified, as he was - like Jesus. Able to stand before God almighty. Able to talk with angels. The mind boggles.

Love In The Room

There are a lot of dark clouds looming in the future, according to almost any forward looking "seer" you might choose to listen to. But the concepts mentioned above blow them all out of the water.

There is no reason to fear a future in which our bodies will be transformed, able to walk on water and slide through solid walls, as Jesus did. There is no need to shudder at a future where God's Spirit, His unconditional love, grace and mercy will be poured out on his people in ways that will astonish even the most sceptical. There is no logic in trembling at a future in which God's own Son will invite us to join him in ruling a new earth and a new heaven.

Sound fantastic? Sound too good to be true? I agree. But I have chosen to listen and believe what God has declared – "For I know the plans I have for you … plans to prosper you and not to harm you, plans to give you hope and a future" (Jeremiah 29:11).

2018. Hallelujah, here we come!

About the Author

Marcia Lee Laycock is an award-winning writer and speaker. Her debut novel, One Smooth Stone, won her the Best New Canadian Christian Author Award and its sequel, A Tumbled Stone was also short-listed for an award. She has written a regular devotional column for over 20 years and has five books in print as well as several ebooks, available Small Pond Press, Amazon and Smashwords.

To sign up to receive Marcia's regular emailed devotionals, or to book her for a speaking engagement, contact her at:

smallpond@telus.net
www.marcialeelaycock.com

www.smallpondpress.com

If you have enjoyed this book, please consider leaving a short review on Amazon.

Made in the USA
Columbia, SC
19 June 2017